To Scott & Angie,
May you derive much
inspiration from this book,
Margret Anne Malsam

MEDITATIONS FOR TODAY'S MARRIED CHRISTIANS

Profiles of Married Saints for Troubled Times

By

Margaret Anne Malsam

D0167687

eaumont Books Inc.

Denver, Colorado

© 1994 by Margaret Anne Malsam

All rights reserved. Printed and bound in the United States of America. No part of this book may be reproduced or transmitted in any form by any means, electronic or mechanical, including photocopying and recording, or by any information storage and retrieval system, except as may be expressly permitted by the 1976 Copyright Act or in writing from the publisher. Requests for permission should be addressed to Beaumont Books Inc., P. O. Box 551, Westminster, CO 80030.

Library of Congress Cataloging-in-Publication Data

Malsam, Margaret Anne
      Meditations for Today's Married Christians -
      Profiles of Married Saints for Troubled Times

      ISBN 0-9616108-8-3
      1. Christian saints - Biography

                                     94-70558
                                          CIP

Computer cover art by Chris Kelson

First Edition / First Printing

DEDICATION

To all who may NOT consider themselves saintly but who are bravely struggling with tremendous family burdens, to those happily married, to those struggling in troubled marriages, to those with failed marriages, and to those considering marriage.

I pray God may bring vibrant new sunshine into all of your hearts and draw you to new heights of holiness.

ACKNOWLEDGMENTS

• Theresita Polzin for her scholarly editing and personal words of encouragement.

• Dolly Lachermeier for encouraging me to continue with my research on married saints.

• Deacon Leonard and Corinne Polak for their keen observations in the Preface.

• Sister Elenius Pettinger for her wisdom and her support and for providing a quiet place for prayer and reflection while completing this book.

• My husband for his patience in bearing the brunt of my absorption in writing the book and for his belief in my ability to complete this task.

• Donna Malsam for her expertise in proofreading.

• To all those who reviewed the book and gave me encouraging comments.

CONTENTS

HOW TO READ THE BOOK

1. Read the Preface, Author's Note, and Introduction to learn more about saints and how they faced their problems.

2. Look through the alphabetical list of categories of married saints according to problems they faced.

3. Select a problem you or a friend are struggling with.

4. Read all the profiles of married saints in that category. Hopefully reading about how they overcame adversities will lighten your heavy loads.

5. Meditate on your specific problem as you read the prayer at the bottom of the page.

6. Pray to the Holy Spirit for guidance and similar courage in your lives.

7. Select another problem and read the profiles, and repeat steps 5 and 6.

8. After you have read through selected profiles according to problems, look through the alphabetical list of married saints and read profiles of saints who especially interest you.

PREFACE

"God created man in his image; in the divine image he created him; male and female he created them." (Gen 1:27). Everyone is created in God's image. This scripture passage contains a very important message to all. We need to listen and to reflect upon the meaning of this text to see how precious human life is.

Our vision today of family is undergoing a dramatic change. The author reflects on married saints in our Church of the past and presents unusual insights about some of the family situations present in our society. You will find the idea of a traditional family being broadened and changed. In the past, the typical family consisted of a man and a woman, married and bearing children.

Now family is the above and more. We have the single parent, the teenage parent, and the professional family in life styles all claiming to be family. The author is showing that in scripture and in the lives of married saints, similar situations existed. She is praying to be compassionate and understanding for all God's creation.

Look at Christ's own words to the woman in John 8: 10-11 where she was being condemned for adultery. "Jesus finally straightened up and said to her, Woman, where did they all disappear to? Has no one condemned you?

'No one sir,' she answered.

Jesus said, nor do I condemn you. You may go. But from now on, avoid this sin." Jesus recognized her uniqueness. He did not condemn the sinner–only the sin was condemned.

The author shows a way to be open to help those in different family circumstances. Her reflections on certain scripture stories along with stories of saints in the history of the Church aid everyone to a deeper understanding of the need for prayer.

Deacon Leonard and Corinne Polak
Archdiocese of Denver, Colorado

Author's Note

One of the hardest tasks for me in writing this book has been selecting saints for this book from a field of nearly 100 married saints. It's like having two or more super qualified candidates for every job opening. Repeatedly I have prayed to God and also asked His saints to intercede in guiding my choices.

The book would be much too long and not nearly as readable if I were to include meditations on the admirable lives of all the married saints and great saints who were never married. Also I realize that there have been many saintly people who lived extraordinary holy lives but who have not officially been recognized as saints.

I do not intend this book of reflections on the lives of married saints to be all inclusive. Rather I encourage you to read further into the lives of other saints–both married and unmarried, lay and religious– and also to study the biographies of courageous people in history who kept God first in their lives.

Abortion, bankruptcy, murder, divorce, unfaithfulness, pregnancy outside marriage, sterility, incapacitating illness, alcoholism, juvenile delinquency, physical and emotional abuse are not new to our times. In the past, others dealt bravely with these same seemingly insurmountable, heart-breaking difficulties and were later declared saints. They achieved their greatness by overcoming great obstacles and fighting against the evils of their time. They fought and won! By examining their lives, hopefully we can learn how to cope with our problems and draw ever closer to God by allowing our lives to be guided by the same spirit of faith, hope and selfless love. Their examples can kindle our imagination, renew our idealism and awaken in us the courage, generosity and desire for holiness in our marriages.

I have spent many hours researching facts for this book, which I started 20 years ago. Slowly I kneaded the information into a "dough" and allowed it to rise before dividing it into feathery light rolls. Hopefully the "rolls" will be easily digested and delightfully consumed by anyone with an appetite for real spiritual food.

My purpose in writing this book is twofold:

• to bring new hope, light and inspiration to many married and divorced people today who are wrestling with the same traumatic problems.

• to draw those in happy marriages even closer to God.

Hopefully, the shining examples of their past lives will guide and inspire today's fathers and mothers, stepfathers and stepmothers, grandmothers and grandfathers, and especially the young people whose lives seem devastated by a myriad of calamities.

After examining the lives of many married saints exhibiting great moral courage, I have selected only the most inspiring and arranged them alphabetically by category so you can quickly find a saint who dealt with problems like yours.

"Nothing is impossible with God," St. Paul tells us. The lives of these God-loving people forcibly testify to this Gospel truth.

The Author

Introduction
WHAT IS A SAINT?
A saint lets the light shine through

A little child stood in a great cathedral on a summer morning. The sunlight streamed through the beautiful stained glass windows displaying the servants of God in bright, brilliant colors. A little later someone asked, "What is a saint?" The child replied, "A saint is a person who lets the light shine through them."

Using this definition, we realize there have been many married people in history who have let the light shine brightly through them. All persons in heaven are saints–not just those 2,000 or more who are officially canonized. "Saints" as defined by *Webster's Dictionary*, are "the faithful departed who died in a state of grace and are believed to be with God." Undoubtedly countless more married people have achieved sainthood than have been canonized because of the long and complicated process. Canonization in the Catholic Church requires a detailed investigation of the person's reputation for holiness, writing done by that person, and (except for martyrs) miracles ascribed to the person's intercession after his/her death.

All called to be saints.

A popular misconception is that sainthood requires one to be too "holy, holy" and is above the attainment of today's husbands and wives. This is not true. We are all called to be saints.

"You shall be holy; for the Lord your God is holy." Lev 19:2. "For this is the will of God, your sanctification. For God has not called us unto uncleanness, but unto holiness." 1 Thes 4:3,7.

The second Vatican Council sought to correct the mistaken idea that holiness is something rare or phenomenal. Pope Paul VI emphasized that holiness is "the normal state of life, elevated to a mysterious and stupendous supernatural dignity." Documents of Vatican II state: "We are all

11

called to holiness. Our holiness lies in our work and everyday life. All the faithful of Christ, of whatever rank or status, are called to the fullness of the Christian life and to perfection of charity."

Holiness, a disposition of the heart

Holiness is not so much a matter of pious practices, but rather a disposition of the heart, "which makes us small and humble in the arms of God–aware of our weakness, yet confident–boldly confident–in the goodness of our Father," says the famous St. Therese of Lisieux, known as the "little flower" because of her promises to send flowers of grace. "I will spend my heaven doing good on earth." Many miracles have been verified through her intercession. The Vatican is currently studying the lives of her parents, Louis and Azelle Gurin Martin, as possibilities for sainthood.

Saints were joyful

Saints were joyful people who accepted whatever came their way. They were not sad even when they were beset with many trials. "A sad saint would be a sorry saint," St. Frances de Sales said aptly. "A glad spirit attains perfection more quickly than any other," St. Philip Neri observed.

Only a few saints were known to practice severe penances or wear sackcloth and ashes, but this is the popular notion we have of saints. This is perhaps due to the fact that the early biographers of saints wrote mostly of their sensational qualities in order to impress and inspire the lay people and also to speed up the canonization process.

Many saints regarded severe penances or austerity as false piety, perhaps rooted in pride, not holiness. They realized that sanctity and extraordinary signs do not necessarily go together, and consequently they did not expect miracles to happen as proof of holiness during one's lifetime.

Most often, however, when we hear *saint*, we immediately visualize a cloistered monk, nun or hermit kneeling solemnly in prayer. We think of *saintly* persons as *solitary* persons who denied themselves any worldly pleasures and who endured self-inflicted penances.

Contrary to this popular belief, the road to sanctity is not dreary, bleak, void of pleasure, rest, joy or satisfaction. Many of the saints enjoyed life and derived satisfaction from the good they did while they were still on this earth. "It is possible to live for the next life and be merry in this," said St. Thomas More, a great husband and father, whose inspiring life story was portrayed in the movie, *A Man for All Seasons.*

Seldom, however, do we hear about saints like St. Thomas More who were married and experienced some of the same joys and sorrows as married people today. We don't know much about the many married men and women who led saintly lives perhaps because these holy married –unlike founders of religious orders–didn't have anyone around long enough to diligently promote their canonizations or validate their good works.

In his book, *On Advantages of Matrimony,* St. Augustine says married women have surpassed many virgins in sanctity. I suspect that the many long nights that fathers and mothers have lovingly and anxiously stood by the bedside of their sick children must have earned them many stars in their heavenly crowns.

Shrines honoring saints

Many shrines have been erected around the world in honor of these saints, especially to Mary, the Mother of God, St. Joseph and St. Anne. One of the most beautiful shrines in honor of St. Anne is the Shrine of St. Anne de Beaupre near Quebec, Canada. This shrine, which has relics of St. Anne, has sponsored a grandmother's club for over 35 years. Members try to emulate the virtues of St. Anne, and dedicate their prayers, especially on Tuesdays, for the intentions of its members–today's grandmothers.

A spiritual network

Praying to saints to intercede to God for you is really a kind of spiritual networking. It's like having friends in high places or selecting professional mentors. When you discover saints who lived and worked in circumstances similar to yours and have now earned their eternal reward, you can identify with those saints and ask them to intercede to God to help you along a similar earthly journey.

The intercession of saints in no way diminishes the unique role of Christ as our mediator with the Father. As the glorified humanity of Christ continues to exercise a saving function in heaven, so also do the saints whose holy lives, faith and good works have placed them in God's presence where they are eternally pleasing in His sight.

Today's saints are everywhere

Today's saints are everywhere. They are people who give generously of their time and self to help others. They may not be as esteemed as Mother Theresa, but they are helping others in their own quiet ways. They are people who have endured great trials, like recovering from alcoholism and drug addiction and are now helping others combat the same problems. Today's saints are those patiently enduring great pain in terminal illnesses. Today's saints are people who practice Christian virtue in a heroic but not necessarily extraordinary way. They are the people who remind us that religion is not a brake but a spur that continually excites us to strive for what is the best and noblest in human nature.

Secrets of the saints

The saints achieved greatness by answering the call to holiness, which is a call for all.They observed the Great Commandment and loved God with their whole being, and they loved their spouse, their children, and their neighbors as much as themselves. Their deep love for God was manifested by prayer and their genuine concern for others as brothers and sisters of God's family. Many of them possessed a great zeal for caring for the poor, sick and the dying. They judged life as Christ would have done and followed His holy and simple example. When they encountered difficulties, they persisted—where lesser men and women might have faltered.

"There is a greatness greater than the greatness of success; and that is the greatness of failure. For that is the greatness of being, without the encouragement of doing; the greatness of sacrifice, of which others less great may reap the fruits," says Archbishop Alban Goodier in *Saints and Sinners.*

The saints were great because they never let adversity destroy their faith or failure destroy their hope nor indifference destroy their love of God and their fellow human beings. They did not let circumstances in their life overwhelm them; rather they became masters of their environments. The fact that these men and women of other centuries could rise above their environments and achieve sanctity in spite of the adverse conditions surrounding them gives hope to today's married Christians

Their lives were marked by the courage to change the evil ways of their time. They had the courage of their convictions, and they were guided and formed by prayer and sacrifice. It made no difference whether they were rich or poor; many saints were just common people. The saints did their jobs without complaint, for the love and joy in serving the Lord. They attained sainthood by giving God and their fellow human beings the best they had to offer.

The saints become saints "because they were patient when it was difficult to be patient...kept silent when they wanted to talk...were agreeable when they wanted to be disagreeable...cheerful when they didn't feel like being cheerful...smiled even though it hurt to smile...yes...even through theirs tears," according to a publication by the monks of Gethsamani in Trappist, Kentucky.

The saints and their eternal reward are aptly described in Revelations 7:15-17: "It was this that brought them before God's throne... Never again shall they know hunger or thirst nor shall the sun or its heat beat down on them...He will lead them to springs of life-giving water, and God will wipe every tear from their eye."

LIST OF MARRIED SAINTS
BY CATEGORY

LIST OF MARRIED SAINTS
AND THEIR FEAST DAYS (alphabetically by name)

Mary, Mother of God
and Help of Christians,
Intercede for me.

ABORTION

Blessed* Gianna Beretta Molla

"No one has greater love than this, to lay down one's life for one's friends."
Jn 15:13

Gianna was a professional 20th century Italian woman who bravely chose life instead of death for her unborn child. She was a normal woman, with a passion for life, for music and for hiking, says her husband, Pietro Molla. At age 39, this woman pediatrician was pregnant when a tumor was discovered in her uterus. Surgery would have meant death for the unborn baby. As a doctor, she knew well the risks she was taking, but she chose to carry the baby to term. She died in 1962 after giving birth to her fourth child.

"Her message is one of the highest respect for life, a message of the Christian life lived out every day with joyful fidelity, enthusiasm and coherence, a message of great faith in Providence," says her husband. He and their four children, including Gianna Emanuel–the child saved by her mother's heroic sacrifice–are still living today in Italy.

Beatified in 1994, this brave professional woman is an inspiring model for pregnant women today whose doctors recommend terminating their pregnancies because of fetus abnormalities or maternal risks. She did not consider murderous abortion as a viable option even though she had valid medical reasons. How many women today choose to abort an unborn child merely "for convenience"?

O Lord, don't let me be tempted to kill one of your innocent ones to protect myself. Don't let me choose murderous abortion just because it is convenient or less risky. Give me strength to endure this pregnancy and accept Your will for myself and the baby as your brave servant, Gianna, did. Even if my unborn baby is not normal, instill in me love for the child. Be with me in this difficult and risky pregnancy.

* "Blessed" is the step before canonization as a saint in the Catholic Church.

ABUSED WIFE

St. Rita of Cascia, Saint of the Impossible

"Keep me as the apple of your eye; hide me in the shadow of your wings from the wicked who use violence against me." Ps 17: 8-9

She is known as the "saint of the impossible" or "advocate of the hopeless" because God has answered her prayers for others so many times. Rita was unhappily married to a mean and unfaithful alcoholic husband who abused her after his drinking bouts. Tearfully, she prayed for his conversion for 18 long years. Finally, he repented, but he had made many enemies and was murdered soon after his conversion.

When Rita learned her two wayward sons planned to avenge her husband's death, she asked God to take her sons from this world (if necessary) before they would commit murder. She loved them so much she would rather see them die than commit such a terrible crime. What a heroic act of mother love.

Her prayers were answered. Before her sons could carry out their evil plans, they became seriously ill. Rita tenderly nursed them and brought them to a forgiving state before they died. Alone in the world, she tried to enter the convent of Cascia, but three times was denied entrance because of the rule allowing only virgins in the order. Finally, the rules were relaxed, and she entered the cloistered convent where she lived for 44 years as a nun. She displayed the same dedication there as she had shown as wife and mother. Her body has remained incorrupt for over 600 years. Many cures have been attributed to her intercession.

O Lord you know how much abuse and heartache I have suffered in my marriage. Like Rita, let me never cease to pray for the conversion of those who hurt me. Bring my husband and children into your forgiving arms.

BURDENED BY OBLIGATIONS

St. Anne Mary Taigi of Italy
"Rejoice in the Lord always." Ph 4:4

Being a mother is not easy in today's world. Being a good and holy mother requires even more grace and wisdom. Anne Mary Taigi is an example of an outstanding example of a devoted wife of 48 years and loving mother of seven.

She loved to pray, and although she was very busy running a household with seven children, she kept very close to God through prayer. She and her husband were poor, but she generously offered what she could to those in need.

She had the gift of prophecy and became known for her good advice. Many people, even bishops and public leaders, came to her for advice because they knew she was close to God.

Through her holy influence, her husband and children were drawn closer to God, too. Her life reflected the truth of the old saying, "The better they served God, the better they served their children."

Help me to be an inspiration to my husband and children. Let me generously share with others even when I do not have much. Give me wisdom so that I may advise others in the best way to serve You and their fellow humans. Let me always seek the right answers through prayer.

BURDENED BY OBLIGATIONS

St. Louis IX, King of France

"Happy the man who remains steadfast under trial, for...he will receive the crown of life which God has promised to those who love Him." Jas 1:12

Noted for his justice, charity, and personal piety, this king of thirteenth century France married a woman who was equally inclined to good works as he was. The marriage was blessed with a happy union of hearts and eleven children. He loved his wife and his children with a true and pure affection. Throughout his marriage, Louis never entered upon any serious undertaking without first consulting his wife. Although the king was burdened by many obligations, he personally instructed the children and selected their teachers.

Louis used his God-given graces and his royal powers for the glory of God. He was every inch a king, but he never let power corrupt him. Rather, he continued to grow in sanctity and good works. The king's charity extended not only to the poor in this country, but also into Palestine and the East. Louis founded numerous religious and educational institutions, including a magnificent chapel in Paris to preserve the sacred memorials of Christ's passion. He looked upon all his servants as brothers and sisters in Christ. He forbade wars among the feudal lords. Often he was sought out as an arbitrator to settle disputes.

Louis embodied the highest ideals of medieval kingship, and France enjoyed unprecedented prosperity and peace during his 44-year reign. A biographer said, "It is only his sanctity that can explain the superhuman results of his reign." On a crusade to the Holy Land, he contracted a fever and died. He was was canonized 27 years later.

Heavenly Father, let me use my talents for your glory as Louis did. Open my eyes to the needs of my spouse, my children, friends, neighbors and fellow workers. Help me respond with generosity to their needs.

BURDENED BY OBLIGATIONS

St. Margaret of Scotland

"Who can find a capable wife? She is far more precious than jewels."
Prov 31:10

She was a great wife and mother whose holy influence changed her husband, her children, and her country in a marked manner.

Married to King Malcolm of Scotland, Margaret exerted a wholesome influence on the king, who passed many good laws. Through her pious influence, the royal court became more civilized, and many new churches were built.

"She excited the king to the works of justice, mercy, alms, and other virtues. For he, seeing that Christ dwelt in the heart of his queen, was always willing to follow her counsels," says her biographer.

The king and queen had a large family—eight children—one of whom would become St. David. Margaret devoted herself to the Christian training of the children, obtaining good teachers for them. Her family was more important to her than reigning as queen. She showed great concern for the poor and needy and encouraged arts and education.

She died soon after learning that her husband and son had been killed by rebels. She was canonized in 1250 and declared patroness of Scotland in 1673.

Lord, let me exert a holy influence on my family and associates. Never let power corrupt me; rather let me use whatever influence I have for the betterment of society.

BUSINESS FAILURE

St. Alphonsus Rodriguez

"God has given and God has taken away. Blessed be the name of the Lord."
Job 1:21

His business failed, he lost his wife and children, but in spite of these discouragements, Alphonsus Rodriguez became a saint. He was the son of a poor wool merchant. He married and became the father of three children. Five years later he was a widower with one surviving child, two others having died previously.

He then began a life of prayer and mortification. After the death of his third child, he desired to enter the Society of Jesus, but was refused. Later he was allowed to enter as a lay brother and spent the last forty-six years of his life as a simple porter or doorkeeper at a Jesuit college in Majorca, Spain. There he earned the deep respect of the many people with whom he had contact. He was a marvelous inspiration to members of his household.

St. Peter Claver followed his advice and developed missions in South America, later becoming known at the "Apostle of the Negroes" because of his work caring for Negro slaves. Alphonsus died in 1617 and was canonized in 1887.

O Lord, when you call those loved ones closest to me on this earth into heaven, do not let me become disheartened. Rather make me realize that I, like Alphonsus, have work yet to do here. Help me befriend the minorities like Alphonsus and to work in my own small way to inspire others to do Your work.

DEATH OF A CHILD

Mary, Mother of God

"Father, into your hands I commend my spirit....All his friends and the women who had accompanied him from Galilee were standing at a distance watching everything." Lk 23:46,49

Although Mary was blessed with many privileges and esteemed more than any other mother, she suffered much. She gracefully endured more sorrows than most mothers, including the ultimate pain of seeing her 33-year old son cruelly beaten, tortured, and sentenced to death on the cross.

Motherhood was more complicated than just caring for his physical needs. She had to conform to the Jewish traditions of the day, such as journeying to Jerusalem every year for the Passover.

She never wavered. She stayed with him until the end. She followed him along the sorrowful Way of the Cross, watching tearfully through all the false accusations and cruelties. She knew her Son did nothing to deserve this kind of treatment. How hard it must have been to see these injustices heaped upon her Son. Even though Mary was spared from sin throughout her life, she was not spared from sorrows.

Lord Jesus, your mother, Mary, endured many sorrows. Help me to smile through the tears of motherhood and prevail through crisis, as she did. Give me the strength to accept the tragedy of the untimely death of my offspring. Send graces to mend my broken heart.

DEATH OF A CHILD

St. Marguerite d'Youville, Religious Foundress
"...do not worry about your life... your Heavenly Father knows your needs."
Mt 6:25,32

Her marriage was not an easy one as her husband was often absent and spent much of his time trading liquor illegally with the Indians. Even though she lived in poverty, she welcomed a blind woman into her home.

She knew the intense pain of losing four of her six young children and a husband, but she did not let personal tragedy destroy her spirit. Rather she devoted herself to alleviating the miseries of the poorest of society. The two remaining children, both sons, became priests, which shows her holy influence as a mother.

Burning with love for God and charity for the poor, this young widow and three humble women started working with the most abandoned members of society–the lepers and incurably ill. These charitable endeavors resulted in the founding of the Sisters of Charity of Montreal (the Grey Nuns) in 1737. She and her sisters suffered many trials. They had to rebuild their hospital after it was destroyed by fire. Because she doggedly fought for the rights of the poor despite much criticism, she became known as the "mother of the poor."

"The saint we honor today had the concrete, everyday charity that makes God's justice triumph," said Pope John Paul II at her canonization in 1990. Her biographer praises "her trust in Divine Providence, her faithful submission to the will of God, and her childlike dependence on the Eternal Father." She is Canada's first native saint.

O Lord, instill in me the strong trust in Divine Providence as Marguerite had. Wipe away my tears in times of sorrow and weakness. Give me strength and courage to start anew.

DEATH OF SPOUSE

St. Jane Frances de Chantal
"There is nothing love cannot face; there is no limit to its...endurance."
1 Cor 13:7

A mother of six, Jane Frances de Chantal of 17th century France, was happily married to a deeply religious and highly educated man, Baron de Chantal, a young French army officer. She kept her household in fine order, but in her husband's absence, she dressed plainly and led a simple life.

Her husband was accidentally shot on a hunting trip, leaving her with four children (previously two had died in infancy). After his death, the young widow went into deep depression. She gave her expensive clothes to the poor and devoted herself to a life of prayer and penance.

Despite the protests of her older son, she desired to enter a convent. She prayed for guidance and met the Bishop of Geneva (St. Francis de Sales) who gave her spiritual direction. Upon his advice, she first provided for the care and education of her four children and then founded a women's religious congregation, "The Order of Visitation." She spent the rest of her life laboring for God in the community.

It was for her and her nuns that St. Francis de Sales wrote his great spiritual classic, *On the Love of God.*

Lord, don't let me be swayed from doing good because others ridicule me. Give me the grace to seek guidance, as Jane Frances did, so that I may know Your will for me.

DESTITUTE

St. Elizabeth Seton, first American-born saint

"Commit your way to the Lord; trust in him, and He will act." Ps 37:5

God came first in her life. She did not allow wealth, social position, even family ties, to become obstacles in her quest for God. She went from riches to rags to eternal glory. Today many wealthy people, like Elizabeth Seton, are suddenly finding themselves penniless. Their wealth had been their identity, and suddenly it's gone–along with their self-esteem. After the death of her husband, her relatives disowned her because she bravely followed her conscience and converted to Catholicism. The once wealthy society matron was left without any means to raise her five children and her husband's orphaned brothers and sisters.

She tried managing a school for boys, but false rumors closed the school. She did not despair. She tried again and founded a girls' school, which became the nation's first Catholic school. This foundress of the American parochial school system and the Sisters of Charity cared for thousands of poor children who came to the school.

She was canonized as American's first native-born saint in 1975. In her life, she experienced the pain of burying a husband, two children, and two stepchildren. Her intercession in heaven obtained a cure for a young Baltimore girl suffering from leukemia.

Lord Jesus, help me realize that material things will not earn me eternal glory nor build true self-esteem and confidence. Guide and strengthen me, as you did Elizabeth Seton, to aspire to higher things. Give me the emotional strength to accept your will and to get going when the going gets tough as Elizabeth did.

DISTRAUGHT STEPFATHER

St. Joseph, Foster Father of Jesus
"Get up, take the child and his mother, and flee to Egypt." Mt 2:13

Being a loving father to one's own child is not easy, but loving someone else's child is even more challenging. In today's society, stepfathers are faced with many trials.

Joseph, like today's stepfathers, provided a home for a child that was not his, and he faced many challenges. Joseph was an ordinary laboring man called to do extraordinary tasks, like fleeing with Mary and the Child Jesus into exile to another country. Then, after the death of Herod, he moved them back to Israel–again according to the angel's instructions.

He was not a powerful man in his society. He was a humble carpenter, and he passed these skills on to his foster son, Jesus.

Joseph lovingly cared for his spouse and her Son, the Child Jesus. Imagine the guilt St. Joseph must have felt when he–the man responsible for the paternal care of Jesus– accidentally departed on the long journey home from Jerusalem without him. How many times do stepfathers make honest mistakes and get bitterly chided for them?

Joseph is a great example of humility and obedience for today's stepfathers. He was given the grace of a happy death, dying in the arms of Jesus and Mary.

Loving Father, grant me the courage and wisdom to discipline and care for my stepchildren lovingly–as Joseph did for the Child Jesus. Let me graciously establish a loving home for my stepchildren. Help me impart a knowledge and love of God in their hearts and protect them against the evils of the world.

DIVORCE

St. Helena, Discoverer of the True Cross

"For I hate divorce, says the Lord God of Israel, so take heed of yourselves and do not be faithless." Mal 2:16

After many years of marriage, one's spouse unexpectedly leaves and seeks a divorce. This happened to St. Helena, who according to tradition, discovered the true cross.

She was married 26 years to a man who coldly put her aside when he became a Roman emperor. She did not let his cruel rejection dampen her spirit or zeal. After the death of her husband, her son, Constantine, became emperor and made her the empress.

A cross appeared in the sky during a battle that resulted in her son's conversion to Christianity and later her embracing of Christianity. Helena went to the Holy Land to search for the cross of Jesus. She tested whether a cross that she found was the true cross by touching a dying person with it. When the person was restored to health immediatley, this confirmed the discovery of the true cross, and she had the Basilica of the Holy Cross built on the spot. She used her influence as an empress to spread Christianity, build other churches and help the poor.

Spirit of God, erase the bitterness from my heart and help me to forgive those who have sinned against me. Heal my deep emotional wounds so that I can smile again, and most of all, trust another human being. Let me use my gifts in your service, as Helena did.

DIVORCE

St. Joan of Valois
"Blessed are the sorrowful; they shall find consolation." Mt 5:4

I know a bright young wife who worked two jobs to help send her husband through law school, but after he became a successful lawyer, he divorced her. Joan of Valois suffered a similar upheaval in 15th century France. When the king was ready to execute her duke husband for political treason, she pleaded for his life, securing a pardon which saved his life. However, after her husband became king, he cruelly tossed Joan aside after 22 years of marriage so he could marry another woman and have an heir to the throne.

Joan, who was physically handicapped from birth, was unable to bear children. Her father had forcibly arranged the marriage of his unattractive daughter to a duke who had always resented the marriage. Even though Joan knew he did not care for her, she had prayed for the success of her marriage and devoted herself to being a good wife.

After the king received his annulment (the marriage had been forcibly arranged by her father), she continued to wear her wedding ring and was very depressed. With God's grace, she exhibited the courage of a saint and forged a new life for herself. She organized charities to help the indigent, visited the poor, and personally administered to the sick.

In the last year of her life, she joined a contemplative religious order she had founded earlier. The first miracle for her 1950 canonization occurred during her funeral. A crippled man who once worked as a gardener for Joan prayed to her to intercede for a healing as her casket passed, and he was immediately healed.

Merciful God, don't let me become bitter when those I have befriended turn against me. Heal my brokenness and help me give my heart completely to You in all that I do.

31

EXILED

St. Macrina, the Elder
Sts. Basil the Elder and Emmelia

"The kingdom of heaven is like yeast that...mixed with flour...(makes) all of it...leavened." Mt 13:33

Holiness, like happiness, seems to be catching in families. Six saints came from one holy Roman Empire family over three generations in the third and fourth centuries.

The saintly matriarch of this family was Macrina the Elder, grandmother to four saints: Basil the Great, Gregory of Nyssa, Peter of Sebaste (all bishops), and Macrina the Younger. Macrina the Elder and her husband suffered many hardships when they were forced to flee into hiding during Emperor Diocletian's persecution of the Christians.

The parents of these four saints, Basil and Emmelia (also canonized saints), were exiled for their Christianity during a religious persecution. Later they were allowed to return with their 10 children to their home in present-day Turkey.

These saintly couples, like many of today's husbands and wives, faced many difficulties. However, with God's grace, they used their problems as stepping stones to holiness.

Lord, since we are "one in flesh" through marriage, help us to become "one in spirit" in doing good works in Your holy name. Let us inspire one another to seek greater spiritual gifts and draw closer to You.

FALSELY ACCUSED

St. Hermenegild
"When I called, you answered me; you built up strength within me." Ps 138: 3

For holding steadfast to his religious beliefs in sixth century Spain, Hermenegild was falsely accused of treason and put to death by his own father, the king of Spain.

Hermenegild had converted to Catholicism through the teaching of St. Leander, archbishop of Seville, and the prayers and example of his zealous wife. When the king disinherited him because of his conversion, Hermenegild resolved to defend himself. The king tricked him into surrendering by promising to forgive him. After he gave up the two-year struggle, the king had him imprisoned and tried to shake his son's faith with both torture and bribes. With fervent prayer, he asked God to give him fortitude to resist.

Hermenegild wrote his father that he would rather lose his life then deny the truth of God. After he repeatedly refused to embrace Arianism, Hermenegild was beheaded on Easter in 585 and later venerated as a martyr.

Spirit of God, give me the strength to hold steadfast to my beliefs. Never let me deny or turn against you. Fill me with complete trust and Your love.

FAMILY FEUD

St. Hedwig
"Blessed are the peacemakers for they shall be called sons of God." Mt 5:9

Although she was the mother of seven, she did not let the duties of raising a large family interfere with her desire to serve God and fellow human beings. She was married to Henry, the Duke of Poland, and together they founded several monasteries and hospitals in the thirteenth century.

Two of her sons warred over the division of lands, and Hedwig successfully intervened between the two, restoring peace to the countries. After the death of her husband, she moved into a Cistercian monastery that she and her husband had founded. Two years later her son, Henry, was killed in a battle.

Many miracles were attributed to her intercession, and she was canonized a saint in 1267. Two of her nieces, Elizabeth of Hungary and Margaret of Scotland, also have been canonized as saints.

Lord, I know there is much dissension in my family. Let me bring peace in my family, serving as a peacemaker as Hedwig did between her two sons. Let me never be too busy with my family responsibilities to help others in need.

FAMILY VIOLENCE

St. Clotilda, the Apostle of France
"Create in me a clean heart, O God, and put a new and right spirit within me."
Ps 51:12

This queen of sixth century France was married to pagan King Clovis. He allowed their first child to be baptized, but the child died in infancy and he used that as an excuse against becoming a Christian. Although he allowed their second child to be baptized, he refused to embrace Christianity.

Clotilda continued to pray for his conversion and practiced penance in secret. Yet she always dressed and acted like the regal queen she was. When Clovis was about to be defeated in a battle, he appealed to "Clotilda's God," promising to become a Christian if he won the battle. He was victorious and was baptized along with his sister and 3,000 warriors. The piety and prayers of one woman resulted in a great victory for Christianity, and Clotilda is known as the "Apostle of France." Her grandson, Cloud, whom she raised, also is a canonized saint.

After her husband's death, she had many trials to endure. Her three sons engaged in family feuds over their inheritance. Tragically her son, Clotaire, killed two of his nephews–her grandchildren. Also her daughters were mistreated by their husbands. She prayed for peace in the family, and her prayers were answered before she died in 545 at the age of 71. She spent the last years of her life in the service of God, caring for the poor and the suffering.

Spirit of God, in the face of disagreements and feuds in my family, instill in me some of the same peacemaking virtues as Clotilda. Grant a new and forgiving heart to those who do violence to others.

FAMILY VIOLENCE

St. Radegund, Patron Saint of Women's Liberation
"Blessed are they who put their trust in Him." Ps 2:12

Radegund's whole life was darkened by savage crimes of violence, yet this sixth century woman rose above them and is known as the patron saint of women's liberation.

Her father, King of Thuringia in Germany, was murdered by his own brother. Twelve-year-old Radegund was snatched as booty by the invading Franks, and Prince Clothar reared her to become a future bride.

As soon as he judged her old enough, he married the beautiful girl, but he turned out to be an unfaithful male chauvinist with uncontrolled passions. She tried to soften his harsh, insensitive pagan ways, but was not too successful. He murdered two of his nephews. He set fire to a hut, burning alive several of his own relatives.

As queen, Radegund lavished money and food on the poor and cared for many of the impoverished herself. She might have continued in this unhappy marriage if her husband had not murdered her brother. This was too much for Radegund. She decided to leave Clothar and asked Bishop Medard to make her a deaconess. When he hesitated, Radegund veiled herself and turned her villa into a hospice for the poor and the sick. When her husband tried to reclaim her, she turned to Bishop Germain of Paris for help. The saintly bishop persuaded the king to grant Radegund her freedom. She maintained cordial ties with her royal in-laws who protected and assisted in her charitable works. After founding two monasteries for nuns, she lived in an adjoining cell and participated in their community life although she did not join the order.

Lord, my burdens are heavy but not as awesome as Radegund's. Give me the courage to rise above my troubles and see them as stepping stones to my sanctification. Let me always trust in You who are always here for me.

ILLICIT SEX

St. Margaret of Cortona
"Many sins are forgiven her, because she loved much." Lk 7:47

Not all the married saints had happy marriages, were of royal families, or had pious parents. Many saints were born into notorious families, had unhappy marriages, and many lived sinful, scandalous lives before their conversion.

Margaret of Cortona of 13th century Italy was involved in an illegitimate relationship with a rich nobleman. When Margaret was a child, her mother died, her father remarried and her stepmother treated her harshly. Unhappy at home, Margaret accepted the enticing offer of a passing nobleman to live in luxury with him. She was a mistress in his castle for nine years, bearing him an illegitimate child. She had fancy clothes and fine jewels, but she was not truly happy because her conscience bothered her. She lacked the courage, however, to break the bonds which chained her.

Her lover journeyed away from the palace to settle a dispute and was killed by a young man. After several days absence, his faithful dog returned and led Margaret to the place in the woods where his master had been buried. Gazing at his corpse, the eyes of her soul were opened and she fell to the ground. She became a changed woman, laying aside her rich robes and disposing of her wealth.

At first, Margaret did penance to atone for her sins. Later she performed penances out of her intense love for God. For this public repentance, historians cite her as a second Mary Magdalene because she had such a great capacity for love. This trait, once her weakness, became her strength– much like Mary Magdalene.

Lord, don't let the lure of riches and illicit pleasures lead me astray. Let me face my sins as Margaret of Cortona did. Transform my passionate nature into love for You.

IMPRISONED

St. Margaret Clitherow
"...a capable wife...Her children call her blessed...her husband sings her praises." Prov 31:10,28

This exemplary wife and mother became the first woman martyr in the reign of Queen Elizabeth. She was canonized by Pope Paul VI in 1973 with 39 other English martyrs who died for their faith during the religious persecution of Catholics in 16th and 17th century England.

She was married to a wealthy butcher who established her in a fine home. Even though she had many worldly goods, she did the humblest household tasks herself for the glory of God. She was a holy Martha—a busy housewife— but she also found time to pray and meditate.

Her lovely home had many secret chambers and passageways, including a chapel where fleeing priests often celebrated Mass. When English authorities searched her home and discovered these hiding places, they imprisoned the whole family. She was expecting another child when she was tried and sentenced to die on Good Friday, March 25, 1586. Her executioners cruelly crushed her to death by placing a heavy door on her and letting heavy weights fall upon the door.

Even if she had not been martyred, her exemplary life as a wife and mother would have been noteworthy. Her heart was filled with love for her husband and children. At the end of the day, she would gather her three little children around her and spend an hour praying and talking to them about God. The two boys became priests, and the girl became a nun.

Lord, give me the grace and wisdom to teach my children about Your wondrous ways as Margaret Clitherow did. Give me the courage to bravely help others in need even though I may suffer for it.

IMPRISONED

St. Thomas More

"Fathers do not anger your children. Bring them up with the training and instruction befitting the Lord." Col 3:21

Refusing to go along with your supervisor's commands takes courage. Because he loved God above all things, Thomas More refused to sacrifice his principles in the workplace. For his dramatic refusal, he was imprisoned and then sentenced to die.

This well-known London lawyer was devoted to his family, which included four children, their spouses and many grandchildren who all lived in his household. After his first wife died leaving him with four young children, he married a second time. Even though he much preferred to be at home among his family, friends and his books, Thomas found himself in a prestigious position on King Henry VIII's royal council in 16th century England.

Truth, reality, and justice were much more important to him than social popularity, worldly honor, and monetary reward. He gave his life rather than take an oath which denounced the Pope as the supreme head of the Catholic Church in England and would enable the notorious King Henry VIII of England to put away his first wife and marry Anne Boleyn. Thomas More gives us a shining example of supreme courage in the workplace and a loving family life.

Spirit of God, when I know that I am right, give me the courage to stand up for my convictionss as Thomas More did. Do not let me become complacent and rationalize away what I know to be wrong. Rather give me the grace to ignore the ridicule of others and hold fast to my principles.

INFERTILITY

Sts. Joachim and Anne, Grandparents of Jesus
"We have waited eagerly for the Lord...our help and our shield." Ps 33:20

Anne and Joachim are revered as the parents of the Blessed Virgin Mary, but they are not nearly as well known as the "grandparents of Jesus." Today's grandparents, some of whom are raising their own grandchildren, have an inspiring role model in Anne and Joachim, who must have bounced the blessed little Jesus, their grandchild, on their laps many times. What an honor to be the grandparents of our Savior and be privileged to hold Him in their arms.

Anne and her husband, Joachim, prayed for a child for about 20 years, but she failed to conceive. While visiting in Jerusalem, Joachim was chided by the high priest for the couple's barren state. On the way home, an angel appeared to him and told him that a daughter would be born to them. The angel foretold Mary's future and the birth of Jesus as the Son of God. Anne also received the same visitation.

Mary's birth, like the birth of John the Baptist to the elderly Elizabeth and Zachary, shows that "nothing is impossible with God." Couples having trouble conceiving a child can pray to Anne and Joachim to intercede with God to send them a child.

The guidance and holy parental influence of Anne and Joachim upon the Blessed Virgin Mary is shown in the gospel when Mary reveals her strong character and decision-making ability as she responds to the angel's troubling announcement of the Incarnation with: "I am the servant of the Lord. Let it be done to me as you say."

Lord, the lives of your faithful servants, Anne and Joachim–your maternal grandparents–give me hope for accepting Your will in raising my grandchildren. Let me tenderly care for their physical needs and joyfully inspire and guide them in Your holy ways.

INFERTILITY

Sts. Zachary and Elizabeth
"Nothing is impossible with God." Lk 1:37

Many times couples who marry later in life long for a child, but are having trouble with infertility. Then they start to believe that they are too old to ever become parents, but they should not lose hope in God.

An angel appeared to Zachary and told him that--at long last--he and his wife, Elizabeth, who both were in advanced age, were to become the parents of a son.

Zachary doubted the power of God. Although his prayers for a child had finally been answered, he refused to believe. As a punishment, he was struck dumb-unable to speak. The angel told him that when the prophecy was fulfilled, he would be able to speak again.

At John's circumcision, Zachary, still unable to speak, was asked what the child's name would be. He wrote on a table: "John is his name." At this moment, his tongue was loosened as he praised the Lord.

That son, born late in life to Zachary and Elizabeth, was John the Baptist, who fulfilled the prophecy as the forerunner of the Messiah.

All-powerful God, let me never doubt your power. Knowing that nothing is impossible through your power as witnessed by Zachary and Elizabeth, please send us a child. If a child is not in your plans for us after many infertile years of marriage, let us not become bitter but joyously continue to proclaim your word.

INTERFERING RELATIVES

St. Adelaide of Burgundy
"You shall not hurt a widow or an orphan." Ex 22:21

When a woman loses a husband, she often loses some of her dignity and place in society. As a widow she is no longer invited to social events attended by couples. Also many times, she is left without adequate funds.

After the death of her first husband, Adelaide was treated with brutality. She was imprisoned for refusing to marry the son of the successor to the throne. She escaped, and King Otto the Great rescued her by marrying her. They had four children.

Her tribulations continued again after the death of Otto who was crowned Emperor of Rome in the 10th century. She was unjustly treated by her son, Otto II, and his wife who turned her husband against his mother, driving Adelaide from the palace. Later the son brought her back, but after he died, the daughter-in-law again cruelly expelled Adelaide from her rightful place in the court. Throughout her trials, however, she continued to be peace loving and generous. After her daughter-in-law died, Adelaide was returned to the palace, and she used her assets to restore and establish monasteries.

Lord help me to gracefully endure the rejections of my relatives who have not been cordial to me since the death of my spouse. Don't let me despair when I encounter rejection as Adelaide did. Whenever I feel social rejection from my own kinfolk or married couple friends, let me put my trust in you, Lord, and not in things of the world.

INTERFERING RELATIVES

St. Elizabeth of Hungary
"Blessed are they who hunger and thirst for holiness; they shall have their fill."
Mt 5:6

After Elizabeth's marriage to the Duke of Thuringia, the court became known for the integrity of its knights and ladies. Her husband and she worked to relieve the weak and the oppressed in their kingdom. Together they advanced in virtue. She preferred visiting the poor and sorrowful to wearing rich garments and taking part in royal ceremonies.

It was a happy marriage filled with romance and holiness. They so enjoyed each other's company that she accompanied him on rugged hunting trips. When she was expecting her fourth child, her husband died. So ended "a union not only of love, but sanctified by piety of heroic degree on the part of both husband and wife," says Father Hugh Francis Blunt in the book, *Great Wives and Mothers*.

After her husband's death, she and her children were driven from the palace into the streets by her brothers-in-laws. Later her estate was returned to her and she was installed in the palace again. She continued to live a life of poverty, giving everything to the poor. After securing places for her children, she took the Habit of St. Francis and dedicated herself to serving God in absolute poverty and humility. After her death, many great wonders were attributed to her intercession, and only four years later, she was canonized a saint.

Please help me, Lord, to grow in love for my spouse as I grow in love for You. I want my marriage to be a holy union like Elizabeth of Hungary's. I want to cherish my spouse as Christ cherishes His Church. Help me forgive interfering relatives and not let them destroy the beauty of my marriage.

43

INTERFERING RELATIVES

St. Matilda

"He has put the mighty from their thrones and exalted the humble." Lk 1:52

Wife of King Henry of Germany, Matilda was the mother of St. Bruno, Archbishop of Cologne. She also was the mother of several sons and daughters who became royalty. During her husband's holy and victorious reign, she lived a life of prayer, establishing many churches and monasteries.

After her husband's death, she was cruelly stripped of her dowry by her relatives. Finally they repented and restored her lawful rights, which allowed her to give even more generously to the poor.

She became known for spreading the glory of God and was venerated as a saint almost immediately after her death in the second century.

O God help me, like Matilda, to inspire my children to achieve their full potential. Let me instill a deep love of God in them that will remain with them always. Help me grow in graces so that I can be a good example. After my spouse's death, give me strength to endure the things that I cannot change and the courage to discover new directions in my life. Keep me always working to build up Your kingdom.

LOST CHILD

St. Joseph and Mary, Mother of Jesus
"When the festival was ended and they started to return, the boy Jesus stayed behind in Jerusalem, but His parents did not know it." Lk 2:43

Joseph and Mary must have been quite concerned for the physical safety of Jesus when they discovered He was not with anyone in their traveling group. Mothers and fathers today fear for their child's well-being when they become separated from their child, even if it is only for a few moments when shopping. A lost child today can be very distressing for parents in these high-crime days. Parents worry about their child's safety from the time they discover the child is missing to the moment they find him or her in the woods or strayed a few blocks from home.

Jesus was lost from His parents for three long days. This must have been a very long, agonizing three days for Joseph and Mary. It must also have been a joyous reunion when they found Him.

Joseph and Mary, like today's parents, must have found it hard to "let go" and treat Jesus as a grownup. When they finally found Him confidently conversing with elders in the temple, Jesus gently reminded them that it was time for Him to be about his father's business. Do we know when it is time to regard our young people as adults?

Dear Lord, help me be a good parent. Let me imitate the loving and patient qualities of Joseph and Mary. Give me the wisdom to know when I should say "no" and when it is time "to let go." Watch over my children, guard their souls, and keep them safe from physical harm. Help me to cope emotionally with the responsibilities of child rearing.

MARTYR

Sts. Felicity and Perpetua

"Blessed are you when people revile you and persecute you....Rejoice and be glad, for your reward is great in heaven." Mt 5:11-12

Twentieth century America, with its emphasis on materialism and worldly pleasures, has been compared to the declining moral culture of the Roman Empire. It's reassuring to note that even though immorality was rampant, many Roman Christians achieved sainthood during that era. If they could become saints in spite of the adverse culture, today's American Christians can do the same.

Felicity and Perpetua were two brave young mothers who were killed for holding fast to their belief in God. Perpetua, a young and beautiful matron, had recently given birth to a small child when she and her pregnant slave, Felicity, were arrested during the persecutions of Christians in third century Rome.

Felicity prayed for deliverance of her child safely and she gave birth to a daughter only three days before her martyrdom. According to Perpetua's writings, the young slave girl endured the pangs of labor so patiently that the jailer was converted to Christianity. The two young Christian mothers were sentenced to die at the public games in the amphitheater. When they were exposed to the wild beasts, however, they remained unharmed so they were cruelly sworded to death.

Instill in me great faith and devotion as Felicity and Perpetua exhibited. Let me never be ashamed of my faith; rather let me boldly declare my belief in You before others so that they may come to know the joy of Your divine love.

NOTORIOUS FAMILY

St Francis Borgia
"...the seed that falls on good ground...yields a hundredfold." Mt 13:23

This saint was born into a notorious royal family in the most unlikely conditions for sanctity in 16th century Rome. He lost his mother at age ten, and his upbringing was as bad as his ancestors had been. In spite of these adverse conditions, he steadily but slowly climbed toward sanctity.

The young duke was a devoted family man and loved his wife and eight children dearly. He liked to hunt, eat well, and he enjoyed good books and music. He was a friend to everyone, including Ignatius Loyola, founder of the Society of Jesus (Jesuits).

After the death of his beloved wife, Francis asked Ignatius Loyola to admit him into the Jesuit order. Three years later after he had provided for the care of his children, he joined the Jesuits. This 'duke turned Jesuit' was the sensation of the day, and the crowds at his first public Mass were so large that it had to be moved outdoors.

He expanded the Jesuit order into several countries and fought against the injustices of the Inquisition. He had a special love for the poor and ignorant, helping to raise alms for victims of the 1566 pestilence in Rome. He attended the sick, gave guidance and consolation throughout the city.

Teach me, Lord, Your ways. Create in me a new heart. Let me blossom in my family and my career– wherever I am placed–as Francis Borgia did. Give me strength to fight against the social injustices of today.

PLAYBOY

St. Hubert

"I found Him whom my heart loves. I took hold of Him and would not let Him go." S of S 3:4

Each of us has an inherent capacity for good and a weakness for evil. "There is a latent potentiality in each sinner to become a saint," says Archbishop Alban Goodier, S.J. in *Saints for Sinners*.

Hubert was a dashing royal lad married to a countess. He was a rich playboy who very much loved a worldly life before his dramatic conversion experience. On a Good Friday morning when everybody else was going to church, Hubert, who loved hunting and is known as the patron of hunters, went out after a stag. In a clearing of the woods, the beast turned, displaying a crucifix between its horns. Hubert heard a voice saying: "Hubert, unless you turn to the Lord and lead a holy life, you shall go down into hell." Hubert got off his horse and got on his knees, asking what he should do. The voice advised him to seek out Lambert, a bishop in France, who would guide him.

Under the discipline of St. Lambert, Hubert was converted. After his wife died, he then renounced all his honors in the royal court and gave his younger brother guardianship of his infant son. After distributing his wealth among the poor, he studied for the priesthood and was soon ordained. He became one of St. Lambert's chief associates.

After the bishop was murdered, Hubert was selected to govern in his place. People traveled many miles to hear him preach the Word of God with zeal and eloquence.

Lord, I want to participate fully in the plans you have for me. Help me to let go of old wrongs and start anew. Wash away my sins and fill me with Your Divine grace.

PREGNANT, UNMARRIED DAUGHTER

St. Anne, Grandmother of Jesus

"The virgin shall be with child and give birth to a son." Mt 1:23

One of my friends is a great grandmother, but her joy is dampened with sadness. She will never get to know or share special moments with her great granddaughter. This child, conceived out of wedlock, was given up for adoption by the 17-year-old mother.

Sadly, more babies are being born outside of marriage, and even more disheartening is the fact that many of these innocent babes are being killed before they are born for the "convenience" of all those involved. At least my friend's granddaughter chose life–not death–for her child.

Anne, as the mother of the Mother of God, is the patroness of women, mothers, and women in labor. Her name means "prayerful one" in ancient Hebrew.

In the small Jewish town, Anne and her husband, Joachim, most likely felt great shame for their daughter, Mary, a noted temple virgin, when her pregnancy began to show. Although they must have suffered greatly, they bore this shame gracefully because they knew they were destined to be the grandparents of Jesus, as the angel had foretold. Their joy must have been mixed with sadness when they realized that their grandchild, the Divine Child, would sacrifice His life for the salvation of all mankind.

St. Anne, you knew the heartache of having a daughter become pregnant before she was married. Please give me the grace to love and support my daughter during her pregnancy and to wholeheartedly love the innocent child when it arrives. Make me aware that my daughter courageously chose life instead of death for this child. Don't let me become a smug and self-righteous grandmother. Let me condemn only the sin–not the sinner.

49

SICK HUSBAND

St. Frances of Rome
"For those who love God, all things work together unto good." Rom 8:28

Frances of Rome was happily married to a wealthy Roman nobleman in the 15th century. During the first five years of their marriage, three of her children died shortly after birth. She had three more children and insisted on caring for them herself instead of entrusting them to a nursemaid as was the custom for women in her position.

Even though she had many household and social responsibilities, this young mother took time to pray and help the city's poor and sick. She was ridiculed for her generous efforts by the townspeople because such charitable works were not considered proper for a noblewoman.

Tragically, two of her children died before reaching adulthood, and she had spiritual visions involving angels after their deaths. During her husband's long final illness, she lovingly stayed by his side. His dying words must have been of great consolation to her: " I feel as if my whole life has been one beautiful dream of purest happiness. God has given me so much in your love."

After her husband's death, she joined the Oblates of Mary, a unique religious community, which she had earlier inspired.

Lord, give me the courage to help those in need as Frances of Rome did. Help me to ignore those who might ridicule my efforts. Keep me steadfast in my love for my spouse and family, always giving them my loving care. Let me realize that God must come first in my life, my spouse and family second, and my career or volunteer work last.

SUBJECTION TO OTHERS

St. Isidore, Patron Saint of Farmers

"...Throughout the earth I give you all plants that bear seed, and every tree that bears fruit with seed: they shall be yours for food. God saw all that he had made, and it was very good..." Gen 1: 29,31

Saints like Isidore bring added dignity to physical labor. His life shows that hard labor and the simple life are conducive to cultivating holiness and happiness.

He was born of poor parents in the 12th century in Madrid, Spain. From the time he was old enough to work as a hired hand until his death, Isidore faithfully toiled the farm of a wealthy landlord. He is known as the patron saint of farmers and rural communities. He arose early to go to church, and then communed with God as he walked behind the plow. He so loved the poor that he shared meals with them, reserving only the scraps for himself. Isidore, like St. Francis of Assisi, also had a genuine love and concern for the proper treatment of animals.

He was married to a woman, Maria de la Cabeza, who was simple and upright as himself. She also has been honored as a saint.

He was declared a saint along with Ignatius, Francis Xavier, Teresa and Philip Neri in 1622. In Spain, these five great servants of God are known as "the five saints." Over the centuries, many miracles have been reported through Isidore's intercession.

Lord, let me never be ashamed of doing repetitive, manual work as your servant, Isidore. Let me offer up my tasks cheerfully as a constant prayer. Help me to grow in grace as I lead a simple life.

TROUBLED MARRIAGE

St. Bathild
"Whoever humbles himself will be exalted." Lk 18:14

Her unusual story is one of rags to riches and back to rags again. Bathild was born a slave girl in seventh century England and taken off to France by slave raiders. At the mayor's palace, she rose quickly in rank from a kitchen maid to a server for the king's table. King Clovis II fell in love with the beautiful little serving girl and made her his queen.

The queen bore three sons, governed the royal household well, and showered alms on the church and the poor. She provided a gracious counterbalance to the uncouth king husband who was a womanizer, a glutton and a heavy drinker.

After the king died, Bathild ruled the kingdom capably and wisely. She established many reforms, such as banning infanticide and the buying and selling of Christian slaves. She lavishly endowed monasteries and shrines and other charitable institutions.

After her oldest son became king, she retired to a cloistered convent, where she did the simplest of tasks with humility and zeal, even cheerfully volunteering to clean the latrines.

Lord, thank you for the many favors you have given me, but never let success spoil me. Keep me steadfast in Your love. Give me humility to do the simple tasks well as Bathild.

TROUBLED MARRIAGE

St. Catherine of Genoa
"For this I know that God is on my side." Ps 56:10

At an early age, Catherine reached a high level of contemplative prayer and expressed an interest in the religious life. At 16, however, this beautiful young girl obeyed her family's wishes and married a shiftless, ill-tempered man for political reasons. She felt nothing but repugnance for her husband, who was unfaithful to her, gambled heavily, and was hardly ever home. For the first five years of her marriage, she kept close to home, quietly increasing her prayers, penances, and good works. Then for the next five years, she emerged into the society of her day, seemingly abandoning her intense religious practices but never her deep trust in God.

After ten years, her husband's extravagance reduced them to poverty. She, like many other saints, was a good influence on her wayward husband. He reformed and joined her in serving the sick and the dying, especially during the plague of 1493 which killed many people.

Following his death, she continued her charitable hospital work and had many visionary experiences. She also cared for her husband's former mistress and illegitimate daughter. After a long and painful illness, she died at age 62. Eighteen months after her death in 1510, her body was untouched by corruption, and she was canonized. Her writings have become outstanding documents on mysticism. She is a good model for today's working women because, for most of her adult life, she worked full-time in a hospital–doing the most menial jobs to being a top administrator.

Lord, stabilize my floundering marriage. Let me be a good influence on my husband and guide him along the right paths. Give me the grace to imitate Catherine of Genoa and forgive the hurts–physical and emotional inflicted upon me.

TROUBLED MARRIAGE

St. Elizabeth of Portugal

"God is our refuge and our strength, an ever-present help in distress." Ps 46:2

As the daughter of an excommunicated king, Elizabeth was born amidst much immorality. At the age of 12, she was given in marriage to King Diniz, an excommunicated king, for political reasons. She bore him two children, but it was anything but a trouble-free marriage. She suffered much due to his unfaithfulness to her. In a letter to her brother, she writes, "O my dear brother, what a life of bitterness I am leading! On whom but God can I lean?"

She rose above her many heartbreaking family difficulties and reached out to make arbitrations to ward off a civil war in Portugal. Later she was successful in establishing peace between her husband and her son after five years of dissension.

In addition to becoming known as the patroness of peace, Elizabeth also had a great regard for the poor and orphaned. She established institutions for orphans, visited the sick, and even administered to lepers. In the midst of her troubles, she turned to God and saw Him in all those whom she helped.

O God, let me rise above my marital troubles as Elizabeth did. Give me hope and don't let my personal marriage or family troubles keep me from helping others. Let me be generous as Elizabeth in helping other. Let me never indulge in self pity or feelings of hopelessness because I have been so wrongly treated.

UNBELIEVER

St. Hilary of Poitiers
"Happy are those who hear the Word of God and keep it." Lk 11:28

Hilary was born into a wealthy pagan family and was converted from paganism to Christianity through his study of the Bible. He was deeply impressed by the sublime description of God given by Moses in the Old Testament and the descriptions of the Divine Word in the New Testament.

After receiving knowledge of the Catholic faith, Hilary was baptized and soon converted his wife and daughter. Later he was ordained to the priesthood. Then, despite his objections, he was made a bishop of Poitiers in 353. He was exiled for three years because of his strenuous defense of the Church against heretical Arian teachings. During his exile, he wrote twelve books about the Holy Trinity. Hilary is known as one of the greatest religious luminaries of France in the fourth century. He died in 368, and in 1851, he was declared a Doctor of the Church.

Let me grow in knowledge of the scripture, as Hilary did, and use this knowledge to spread Your word. When I am propelled into a leadership role, guide and direct me along the right paths.

UNBELIEVER

St. Paulinus of Nola
"I am content with weakness; when I am weak is then when I am made strong."
2 Cor 12: 10

After retirement, Paulinus of Nola discovered God was calling him to begin a new vocation. This pagan lawyer and poet had been a prominent Roman senator before he retired with his Spanish wife to a life of leisure. After seeing several sick people healed at the shrine of St. Felix, he felt the first stirring of divine grace. His conversion by contagion was due to numerous factors: philosophical talks with bishops, seeing St. Augustine and others converted to Christianity, and the prayers of his Christian wife, Theresa.

At about this time, a son was born to them who died shortly after baptism. Soon afterward the couple disposed of their wealth, giving the money to the poor and dividing their property among their slaves.

The people of Barcelona were so impressed with his relinquishment of his high position and worldly goods that they begged the bishop to ordain this holy man into the priesthood. Later, by popular demand, he was ordained bishop of Nola in 409. Paulinus and Theresa established a hospice for the poor and needy in their home. They had a wide circle of friends, including St. Martin of Tours, St. Augustine, St. Ambrose and St. Jerome.

Don't let me ever retire from doing good for you, Lord, because of my age. Give me courage to continue to do your work as Paulinus whose religious life started after his retirement.

UNWED MOTHER-TO-BE

Mary, Mother of God

"When his mother Mary was engaged to Joseph, but before they lived together, she was found with child through the power of the Holy Spirit." Mt 1:18

Graciously Mary accepted God's invitation to become the Mother of Jesus. In lovingly saying "yes" to the angel, she accepted all the problems associated with pregnancy, childbirth and mothering. Just because Mary was sinless from the moment of her conception didn't mean that she was stress free. She–like young unwed girls today– must have been fearful about the changes in her body and apprehensive about the upcoming birth.

Mary, a holy virgin and respected young maiden, must have been disturbed wondering how she would explain her pregnancy to her espoused husband, her parents, and people in the community. An angel later appeared to Joseph, her husband-to-be, and told him to have no fear to take Mary as his wife because the child she was carrying was miraculously conceived through the power of the Holy Spirit.

Even though she was still a virgin and knew she had done nothing wrong, undoubtedly she was the victim of cruel gossip. She must have experienced a humiliating sense of shame in the small Jewish community when her body started to swell with the unborn babe so very soon after she became Joseph's wife.

O Lord, help me, an unwed mother, love the tiny being growing inside me. Don't let me do anything to harm this child. Help me to endure the stinging remarks of friends and family. Give me the grace to become a better and holier person --not a bitter person. Help me prepare for the birth of this child and to become a loving mother like Your own earthly mother, the Blessed Virgin Mary. Please have mercy on me and forgive my past sins.

VICTIM OF GOSSIP

Sts. Henry II and Cunegundes

"Release me from the snares they have hidden from me, for you are my refuge, Lord." Ps 31:5

Those that gossip viciously about others reveal a lack of charity and a mean streak of jealousy. Psychologists tell us that gossips try to build themselves up by tearing down others.

Instead of rejoicing over another's success, gossips spread untrue rumors in an attempt to discredit others. This happened to a husband and wife saint, Henry II and Cunegundes. They were doing many works of charity among the poor, the sick, and the lepers, which had made them many friends.

Jealous people started vicious gossip about Cunegundes in an attempt to cause a rift between her and her husband. She asked for a trial by fire, according to a local custom in 13th century Poland. To prove her innocence, she walked barefoot over red-hot metal and was not burned. Later, after her husband's death, she sold all her possessions and spent the rest of her life in a religious community. This holy royal pair are buried together in the cathedral he had built at Bamberg, Germany.

Teach me to hold my tongue so that I do not speak falsely against another. When others gossip about me, let me not return the insult by uttering unkind remarks about them. Make me realize that those who gossip are lacking in self-esteem or they would not try so hard to tear down another person. Do not let me become discouraged doing good when I know others are spreading false rumors about my efforts.

WAYWARD CHILD

St. Bridget of Sweden
"You have loved right and hated wrong; so God has anointed you with the oil of gladness." Ps 45:7

Bridget of Sweden, a mother of eight, had a great love for the poor and did many works of charity. Her fine works and good example inspired her husband, Prince Ulf, to perform works of charity also. The young mother devoted herself to the care and education of her children. A daughter became St. Catherine of Sweden, but a wayward son brought her much pain.

After her husband died, she founded a religious order (the Bridgettines) in the 14th century. Throughout her life, she experienced remarkable visions, which she wrote about in her *Revelations*. She reformed monasteries and was quite outspoken, denouncing the king and queen for their frivolous lives. She encouraged the pope to return the papacy to Rome and to mediate peace between England and France. When her married son, Charles, became romantically involved in a scandalous relationship with the Queen of Spain (also married), she prayed unceasingly. Her son was struck suddenly with a fever and died in her arms.

Her daughter, Catherine, married a devout young nobleman, and they both spent much time in prayer and works of charity. When widowed at a young age, she repeatedly refused marriage offers by persistent suitors. Instead she joined the same order her mother had founded, becoming her constant companion for the next 25 years. After her mother died, Catherine became head of the convent.

Lord, let me set a good example for my husband and family. Don't let me tire of helping others. Instill in me a cheerful heart and a willing spirit. Give me the courage to speak out against evil in high places, as Bridget did.

WAYWARD CHILD

St. Monica, Patron Saint of Mothers

"Let us live honorably as in daylight, not in carousing and drunkenness, not in sexual excess and lust, not in quarreling and jealousy." Rom 13:13

In his famous *Confessions* book, St. Augustine tells of his sinful sexual exploits and shows how divine mercy led him to repentance and conversion.

Some say that behind every great man is a great woman. St. Augustine's mother, Monica, a mother of three, prayed for his conversion for 17 years. She was married to a harsh pagan man with a violet temper, and she had a troublesome pagan mother-in-law who disliked her from the very beginning of her marriage. Still Monica remained gentle and patient. She attended Mass daily, and despite her husband's objections, she gave generously to the poor. Her son, Augustine, fell in with bad companions and led a dissolute life. He became involved with a concubine who bore him a son.

To further compound Monica's sorrow, Augustine joined a Manichaean heretical sect that denied the influence of God, declaring that right and wrong should be determined by human reason alone. Monica continued to pray for the conversion of both her son and her husband, who converted to Christianity on his death bed. Slowly Augustine became impressed by the clarity and simplicity of the Christian doctrine and abandoned the heresy, but he could not conquer his illicit sexual passions until he read and pondered St. Paul's advice to the Romans. Then joyfully he told his mother that now he belonged to God.

Lord, I keep praying for the conversion of my loved ones as Monica did. Bring out the goodness that lies deep within them. Turn them away from their evil deeds, especially sins of the flesh. Draw them into your protective bosom. Guide and inspire them a desire for higher things.

READERS' COMMENTS (See also back cover)

"We were particularly touched by the situation of Blessed Gianna Beretta Molla, who did not chose to abort her unborn child. Our daughter, Dona, was taking several medications for epilepsy when she became pregnant. Her neurologist wanted her to have an abortion because one of the medications had caused birth defects in laboratory animals. She chose, instead, to have her child, and so today we have her Kevin, who was born without defects and has brought much joy to our lives."

Phil and Edie Vigil, Denver, Colorado

"The brief accounts will be helpful for meditation for Christian people and should help married people...see the joys and problems of married life are universal–extending to all places and times and that the Church has formally canonized many people as saints who have experienced them (joys and problems)."

Rev.David Stahl, St.Catherine's Church, Denver Colorado

"There's a lot of help for married people who are troubled, especially in the meditations. Those who read it will find it helpful reference material when they have problems."

Hugh and Roberta Mellen, Knoxville, Tennessee

"It makes you realize that all times have been tough for married Christians. It gave us so much hope to go another day and to face another problem."

Joe and Dolly Lachermeier, Northglenn, Colorado

"The book is excellent for any family to keep as a reference for meditation to help with daily struggles on the journey of faith. Also, parents could read one saint per day to their children in order to familiarize them with the great saints of the past and the trials they suffered then and are so similar today. Reading only the mediations each day would not take much time and could encourage us to improve our daily lives."

Bill and Helen Eschbacher, Sedalia, Missouri

"There is so much to think about and meditate on in the book. We came away with new patron saints for specific situations and especially enjoyed the analogy in the Introduction about spiritual networking."

Jim and Cyrene Brozovich, Northglenn, Colorado

READERS' COMMENTS (continued)

"It's nice to know that we have saints who were married and had some of the same problems people today encounter. Too often people think of saints as being only applicable to ancient times."
Jeary and Eldi Ingrum, Colorado Springs, Colorado

"The scriptures and prayers add depth to the stories. The book is inspiring because we can see that these people were able to serve Christ and others in spite of their circumstances. Many times we feel alone in a situation, and it is somehow comforting to know that others have faced the problems we are experiencing. We think that the problems of our society as so monumental, but we see that 'there is nothing new under the sun.' "
Jay and Cindy Krebs, Denver, Colorado

"The book is a beautiful and easy-to-read depiction of centuries of human behavior–both good and bad. We are convinced that your book will be an inspiration and encouragement for readers who are struggling with any of the problems categorized."
Andy and Lorna Keller, Santa Maria, California

"The book is inspirational and will be of great help to many because it applies to the world today. It is something that is really needed. We found some powerful messages in it that helped us through a problem we were facing."
Charles and Virginia Auge, Denver, Colorado

"I feel the people who read the book will be helped in their struggles...it (the book) is very well done."
Sister Mary Keller, S.S.J., Concordia, Kansas

"The book illustrates the humanity in all of us and helps us focus on the Lord's understanding and forgiveness – a reminder that Jesus meant what He said."
Fred and Fran Jarigese, Westminster, Colorado

"The book is a most prayerful reflection about saints–each with a different accent; each reflects the brightness of God's light from a different direction–the married vocation. The book is a celebration of new friendships and other likenesses to the image of God."
Robert and Celine Henderson, Denver, Colorado

"The author did a wonderful job on writing about different saints...a very interesting book."
Sister Renilda Keller, S.S.J., Concordia, Kansas

READERS' COMMENTS (continued)

"In my judgment, this is a work beautifully and thoughtfully done. The prayers at the end of each biographical sketch are especially well done and impressive–to the point."

Theresita Polzin, Denver, Colorado

"In this book, married Christians have an inspirational, beautifully-done resource to guide them in spiritual meditation. By relating saints lives to specific struggles, the author enables today's families to identify with saints who lived in the past and also to impress upon us, once more, that all can be accomplished through God's love."

Al and Jo Ann Vasquez, Denver, Colorado

"The author is to be lauded for producing a handbook for meditation and inspiration for today's married persons. An antidote for the scarcity of role models for married people is a great need for our Church and our world."

Sister Elenius Pettinger, O.S.F., Retreat Director
Queen of Peace Oratory, Denver, Colorado

"I have been greatly inspired by the book, and I plan to use it for reference and prayer. The prayers at the end of each history are very applicable to the real life situations of today."

Bernita R. Caesar, Arvada, Colorado

ABOUT THE AUTHOR

Margaret Anne (Hula) Malsam is a wife, a mother, and a grandmother living in Denver, Colorado. She has over 200 credits in

major newspapers and magazines, including GUIDEPOSTS, CATHOLIC DIGEST, OUR SUNDAY VISITOR, and COLUMBIA. She wrote the book, *CAMPING CIRCUS: An entertaining and informative guide to family camping,* (Beaumont Books $6.95) after camping for 10 years with her husband and four children. She is a former DENVER POST writer and worked 15 years in advertising/public relations.

ORDER FORM

Do you know of someone who could benefit from reading this book? We can send them a copy with a gift card from you.

Enclosed is $7.50 for each book postpaid. Please send gift card from _____

Send book to:

Name_____

Address_____

City, State, Zip_____

Mail to: Beaumont Books, PO Box 551, Westminster, CO 80030

Enclosed is $7.50 for each book postpaid. Please send gift card from _____

Send book to:

Name_____

Address_____

City, State, Zip_____

Mail to: Beaumont Books, PO Box 551, Westminster, CO 80030

Enclosed is $7.50 for each book postpaid. Please send gift card from _____

Send book to:

Name_____

Address_____

City, State, Zip_____

Mail to: Beaumont Books, PO Box 551, Westminster, CO 80030